KILLER CREATURES

SPIDER

18

DAVID JEFFERIS
AND
TONY ALLAN

Belitha Press

◀ This is the hairy Chilean rose spider, from South America. In real life, the spider is not quite as big as it appears in this close-up photograph. But it's still a monster, about the size of your hand!

First published in the UK in 2001 by
Belitha Press
An imprint of Chrysalis Books plc
64 Brewery Road, London N7 9NT

Paperback edition first published in 2002

Design and editorial production:
  Alpha Communications
Educational advisor: Julie Stapleton
Picture research: Kay Rowley

ISBN 1 84138 303 1 (hardback)
ISBN 1 84138 382 1 (paperback)

British Library Cataloguing in Publication Data for this book is available from the British Library.

Printed in Hong Kong

10 9 8 7 6 5 4 3 2 1

Acknowledgements
We wish to thank the following individuals and organizations for their help and assistance and for supplying material in their collections:
Alpha Archive, Heather Angel, Ardea London Ltd, BBC Natural History Unit, Jane Burton, John Clegg, David Fox, Harry Fox, Fuji film, Bob Gibbons, Pascal Goetgheluck, Nick Gordon, Daniel Heuclin, Steve Hopkin, Hans Christian Kappel, Fabio Liverani, Brian Kenney, M&C Photography, Mantis Wildlife Films, Steven D Miller, John Mitchell, C Allan Morgan, P Morris, NASA, Natural History Museum, Andy Newman, NHPA Natural History Photographic Agency, Oxford Scientific Films, Hans Pfletschinger, Planet Earth Pictures, Premaphotos Wildlife, Ken Preston-Mafham, Still Pictures, Kim Taylor, Warren Photographic, Woodfall Wild Images

CONTENTS

LOOK FOR THE SPIDER BOX

Look for the little black spider in boxes like this. Here you
will find extra spider facts, stories and other information.
*Note: spiders in this book are shown bigger than life-size,
so you can see them in detail.*

SPIDER WORLD

Spiders live in jungles, deserts, grasslands, marshes and in our homes and gardens. One species even lives underwater.

▲ Spiders have existed longer than humans. This one is thought to have lived nearly 40 million years ago.

There are an awful lot of spiders – over 35 000 different kinds, or species, with more still to be discovered. In some places, a piece of land the size of a soccer pitch is home to more than a million spiders.

Spiders have been around for a long time. Scientists believe that the first spider-like creatures lived about 400 million years ago, which makes the spider family almost twice as old as the dinosaurs.

Today spiders are found almost everywhere – there are probably some near you, right now!

◄ The water spider spins a cocoon of silk under the water. The spider then fills it with air from the surface.

🕷 SPIDER OR INSECT?

Some people confuse spiders with other 'creepy crawlies', and think they are insects. But it is usually easy to tell the difference between an insect and a spider – simply count the legs. An insect has six legs, a spider has two more – eight legs.

Spiders belong to a class of creatures called arachnids, along with scorpions and some mites.

all spiders have eight legs

▶ It's easy to see why the Mexican red-knee spider has its name! The body of this spider is about as big as your hand.

abdomen

SPIDER BODIES

Spiders come in many colours, shapes and sizes. But big or small, they all have the same body parts.

▲ Silk is made inside a spider's abdomen.

Spiders have two parts to their bodies. The front part carries the legs. Inside it is the stomach, eyes and a tiny brain. The larger, rear part is called the abdomen. It holds the heart, lungs and the body organs that make silk. All spiders make silk, but they don't all make webs.

Spiders usually have six or eight eyes, which give a wide view – in fact, the jumping spider can see what's behind without even turning round!

 MOULTING TIME

We have bones inside our bodies, with a soft skin outside. Spiders have no bones, just a hard outer casing like a suit of armour, called an exoskeleton.

Spiders shed their skin up to ten times as they grow, in a process called moulting. Each time they grow too big for their skin, it cracks open, revealing a new casing already grown underneath.

Spiders are not alone in shedding skin. Many creatures do it, including snakes.

► The beach wolf spider hunts for insects on seaweed, rocks and plants. Its colour blends in with pebbles on the beach.

the wolf spider has two big eyes, with four smaller eyes in a second row below

the wolf spider can see for about 30 cm, which is good for a spider

WEAVING A WEB

Only about half of the many spider species build webs. The spiders that do make webs create them in many different sizes and shapes.

▲ Arabella was a spider placed aboard a rocket, to see if she could weave a web in space. She did, but it was rather wobbly.

Depending on the spider that made it, a web might look like a circular net, a sheet lying on the ground, or a hammock slung between bushes or twigs. Some spiders make a web that is just a single strand thick.

Webs are spun from silk, which a spider makes inside its body as a runny paste. The silk is squeezed out like toothpaste through tubes called spinnerets. The silk is about three times tougher than steel of the same thickness.

A well-made web can support up to 4000 times the weight of the spider that built it. Special oil on the spider's feet and body stop it from getting stuck in its own web.

◄ The golden web spider weaves a huge web, up to two metres across. The web is so strong that it has been used as fishing line by Pacific islanders.

◄ Wheel-shaped webs are spun by a group of spiders called orb weavers. Here, early morning sunlight makes overnight dew shine like diamonds.

DIFFERENT SILKS

Spiders make different kinds of silk, for spinning a web, wrapping eggs in a cocoon or tying up prey. Silk is made sticky or not, as needed.

SETTING A TRAP

▲ The trapdoor spider digs a burrow up to 40 cm deep. Side tunnels store food and baby spiders. Some tunnels have false bottoms, for hiding from enemies, such as giant centipedes.

Some spiders use special tricks to trap prey, rather than just waiting for insects to come to their webs.

The trapdoor spider digs a silk-lined burrow, topped with a hinged door. The spider waits inside until it hears an insect scuttling on the ground above. Then it opens the door quickly, bites its prey, and drags the paralysed creature into the burrow.

The web-throwing spider hangs from a tree at night. When an insect passes underneath, the spider drops its web, trapping the insect in a sticky net.

Angler spiders also wait on trees for passing insects – usually moths. But their web is a single length of silk, with a sticky blob on the end. When a moth flies near, the angler spider swings its line to catch the moth on the blob.

WATCH THOSE NASTY JAWS!

Spiders have sharp fangs to bite their prey. They cannot swallow food whole. Instead, they have poisonous juices in their venom. This slowly dissolves the prey's body – and then the spider can suck it up as a nourishing liquid. A spider does not always eat a captured animal at once. Often the prey is wrapped in a silk cocoon to eat later.

▲ An Australian web-throwing spider waits for an insect to pass underneath. At the right moment, the spider will drop its sticky net. Moments later the prey will be bundled up in a silky cocoon.

the Australian web-throwing spider makes its web in a small plate shape, just right for dropping short distances

HUNTING SPIDERS

Most spiders that don't spin webs hunt for prey. Spiders kill by biting. Poison, or venom, flows through their sharp fangs, paralyzing the victim.

the lynx spider spider bites prey to paralyse it with venom.

▲ The lynx spider hunts insects on plants, and will jump from leaf to leaf when chasing prey.

The most common hunters are jumping spiders, named because they stalk prey and then pounce like cats. There are about 4000 different kinds. They are found all over the world, but especially in hot, tropical places. Some can leap 40 times their own body length, putting humans to shame – the Olympic long jump record is 8.95m, less than five times the athlete's body length.

FEELING, TASTING, HEARING

A spider has to hunt prey, but it does not have ears, a tongue or a nose. Instead, it has sensitive hairs over its legs and body, and these let it touch, taste and hear things. The hairs feel vibrations from noise in the air, which tell the spider what is going on around it. Other hairs detect air currents, while the spider's legs have slits that pick up vibrations from movement, such as those of a struggling insect in a web.

▼ A jumping spider leaps after its prey, a hoverfly. You can see the safety line which the spider has attached to the flower.

HIDE AND SEEK

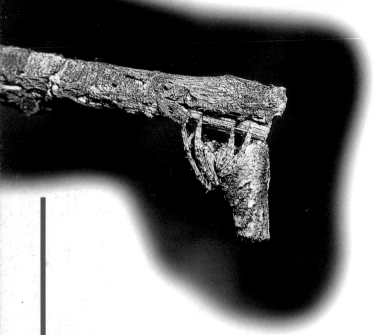

Camouflage is used by spiders so that they can hide from their enemies and wait to ambush approaching prey.

◄ There are all sorts of camouflaged spiders. This twig spider of Western Australia tucks its legs up to look like a bit of twisted wood.

One way to hide is by blending into the background. So leaf spiders are usually green and sand spiders are the same colour as a shingle beach. There are spiders that look like twigs, tree bark, dead leaves – even a spider that looks like a bird dropping!

The ant-mimic spider looks like an ant, but with eight legs, instead of six. Birds and other creatures keep clear because they know that ants often have painful stings.

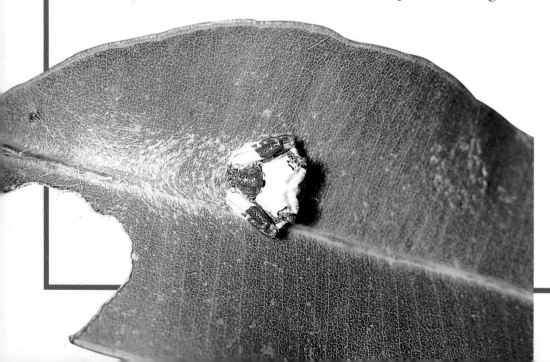

◄ Enemies leave this Australian spider alone. It is disguised as a foul-smelling bird dropping.

most crab spiders are small, about 20 mm long

🕷 CHANGING COLOUR

Crab spiders come in many different shades, and usually choose to hide in flowers which match their colour. Some crab spiders can also change colour, like a chameleon.

The female flower spider changes from white to yellow over about two days. She does this by shifting yellow material from the inside to the outside of her body.

▲ There are about 3000 kinds of crab spider. This one hangs on to the flower with its back four legs while it grabs prey with its front four.

15

WHEN SPIDERS MEET

▲ A male meadow spider walks on tiptoe as he approaches the female. He waves in a special way to attract her.

Spiders usually meet only when they mate. This can be a dangerous time for male spiders, as females are big and hungry.

As a male spider approaches a female, he has to be careful. If she is not ready to mate, or thinks he is an enemy, she may attack!

Some males make signals to show they mean no harm. The male web-weaver plucks the female's web, while the male buzzing spider bangs the back of his body on a leaf.

◄ The golden orb spider may be the safest male of all. He weighs 1000 times less than the female and is too small to be worth eating! Look inside the ring to see the tiny male on the left.

▲ A male wedding-present spider brings a wrapped insect as a gift to the larger female.

Other male spiders bring the female a dead insect as a present. If she is busy eating the gift, she won't eat her mate.

After mating, most males are safe, although the black widow sometimes eats the much smaller male.

 A SHORT LIFE

Many spider species live just one season, so having babies every year is vital. Other spiders live longer. In the wild, tarantulas may live for two to three years, but when kept safely as pets, some have lived 25 years.

BABY SPIDERS

▲ The wandering spider covers up her eggs with bits of dead leaves.

Spiders lay lots of eggs, sometimes thousands at a time. The baby spiders are called spiderlings.

A spider usually lays her eggs a week or two after mating. She takes good care of the eggs so that they will not be eaten by other creatures.

Some wandering spiders carry their eggs in loose bundles. Other species, such as the wolf spider, wrap their eggs in a silk cocoon.

After the eggs are laid, many spider mothers go off and leave them. In some species, the mother stays with her eggs until she dies in the autumn. Next spring, her dead body provides food for the newly-hatched spiderlings.

HATCHING TIME

Orb-weaver spiderlings start to move off, after hatching on a flower head. At this age – just a few hours old – most spiderlings look alike. They start making silk and venom only after they have moulted for the first time.

▶ The tarantula's young turn brown as they grow. Several changes of skin are needed as they get bigger. A cast-off skin is called a cuticle.

these spiderlings have moulted once and now look like tiny adults

GIANT SPIDERS

The biggest spiders live in hot countries around the world. In all, there are about 800 different species.

The really huge and hairy spiders go by several names – tarantula, bird-eater, baboon spider or horse spider.

They may be frightening to look at, but most tarantulas are quite timid. Even so, they have large fangs. Luckily, the venom is not normally strong enough to kill an adult human.

Many tarantulas live in burrows, others live in trees. To help them climb, they have hairy brushes on the ends of their legs for extra grip.

▲ A young chick makes a big meal for this tarantula. More usual prey includes mice, lizards, frogs and small snakes.

▼ The goliath bird-eater is the world's biggest spider. It can give a nasty bite, with fangs that punch down like a staple gun.

back legs flick body hairs like sharp darts at enemies

▲ Tarantulas have poor eyesight, and use sensitive body hairs to detect prey. If attacked, the tarantula can use its back legs to brush off body hairs and flick them at the enemy! This tarantula comes from Mexico.

🕷 WOLF OR TARANTULA?

The true tarantula is not a hairy monster, but a wolf spider from southern Europe. It was named after the town of Taranto in Italy, where workers in the vineyards once feared its bite.

In fact, the creature with the bite may have been the smaller malmignatte spider that also lived in the vineyards. It was much harder to spot, so the tarantula was blamed instead.

DEADLY TO HUMANS

▲ The black widow likes to nest in quiet places such as this – high up in the corner of a barn.

Almost all spiders use venom when they bite, but only about 30 species are really dangerous to humans. Here are two of them.

The black widow from the USA is only 25 mm long, but its venom is 15 times stronger than that of a rattlesnake. The black widow is shy, but attacks if threatened or if its web is disturbed. Only the female is dangerous – the male is so small that its fangs cannot pierce human skin.

The funnel-web spider comes from Australia. It has hairy legs, but a smooth body. It makes a big, funnel-shaped web that stretches out from a burrow. Its sharp fangs can cut through a small animal's bones – and human flesh.

◀ The funnel-web spider can dig a burrow, but mostly uses cracks or holes in the ground. Funnel webs are fierce and can give several vicious bites.

the black widow has an hourglass-shaped mark on its back

► For humans, a black widow's bite is very painful and causes muscle cramps and breathing difficulties. For its prey, a bite means sudden death.

BITE ME – I DON'T CARE!

A black widow's bite is very dangerous for most creatures, but some animals seem to hardly notice it. Sheep and rabbits can be bitten without harm. Their bodies may have a natural cure for the poison, or perhaps thick wool and fur gives them protection.

if a leg is broken, a spider simply grows a new one

SPIDERS AT RISK?

Being scared of spiders is so common that it has a special name – arachnophobia. Yet spiders keep down insect pests and are even used in medicine.

▲ Common house spiders like this one help keep homes free from flies, which carry disease.

Spiders are often killed by mistake – when people cut down the rainforests where many spiders live, or when crops are sprayed with insecticide. Spider collectors want red-knee tarantulas so much that few are left in the wild.

About 20 species are thought to be at risk, but the whole spider family is not in danger. Many scientists say that spiders are better survivors than we are. They have already existed for 400 million years, and in that time have coped with many disasters, from earthquakes to ice ages.

▲ The ladybird spider is a species in danger. This is a male – the female is three times bigger and coloured grey-black.

the male has spots like a ladybird

🕷 MEDICINE OLD AND NEW

Thomas Muffet was the father of 'Little Miss Muffet', the girl who was frightened by a spider in the nursery rhyme. Her dad gave her crushed spiders as medicine when she was ill, so it's no wonder she didn't like them!

Today, spiders are being used again for medical research. The venom of the Chilean rose tarantula (right) can be used to treat people with heart and brain disease.

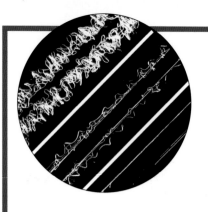

SPIDER FACTS

Here are some facts and stories about the world of spiders.

▲ New silk looks like spaghetti. It straightens out when stretched to make a web.

Long haul
The silk in a garden spider's web would stretch the length of a tennis court if it was unravelled in a single strand.

On a roll
The golden-wheeling spider, which lives in the desert, gets its name because it escapes enemies by curling up and rolling down sand dunes.

Watch out – wasp about
The tarantula hawk wasp is a deadly enemy of big spiders. It paralyses a spider with one jab of its sharp sting. It then drags the helpless spider to its burrow. The body is used as food for the wasp's young.

Big bang
In 1883 a volcano exploded on the island of Krakatoa, in the Pacific Ocean. The explosion killed off all life there. The first creatures to return were spiders, carried by the wind from land 40 km away.

Lightning fast
The fastest hunting spider can run 33 times the length of its body in a second. Human sprinters run about five times their body length in that time.

Biggest spider
In 1998 a Scottish spider fan bred a goliath tarantula with a leg-span of 280 mm.

Smallest spider
The smallest spider is so tiny you can barely see it. The body of patu digua is 0.37 mm long, smaller than this full stop.

MAKING A WEB
An orb spider makes a web in stages. First it gets the top line in place by releasing a sticky thread. The spider creeps along the line, adding a second line for strength. It carries on step-by-step until the web is finished.

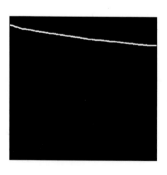

1 A bridge line is swung across a gap.

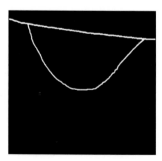

2 A loop line swings under the bridge.

Most deadly spider

The Brazilian wandering spider produces the most poison. It has enough venom to kill more than 200 mice.

Spider cafe

In some places, people eat spiders. A researcher had a taste when living with South American tribespeople. He said that the hairy legs of a goliath tarantula tasted, 'slightly fishy, like prawns'.

▲ Huntsman spiders, live in hot places such as Australia, though they sometimes turn up in cool countries, hiding in fruit boxes! This one has a body 35 mm long.

Wound up

In the old days, people sometimes used spiders' webs as bandages, to stop blood flowing out of wounds.

Spider groups

There are about 35 000 known kinds of spider, which are divided into groups. The biggest groups include money spiders (3700 species), orb-web spiders (2600) and crab spiders (3000). There are more jumping spiders than any others – this group has more than 4000 species!

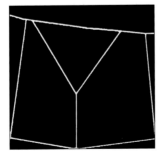
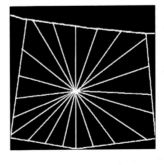
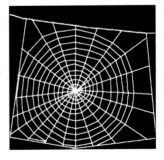

3 A bottom thread makes a Y-shape.

4 Bottom and side threads are added.

5 Threads are spun like spokes of a wheel.

6 The spider finishes with a spiral thread.

SPIDER WORDS

Here are some of the technical terms used in this book.

▲ A crab spider's colouring gives it perfect camouflage on this flower head.

abdomen
The large rear part of a spider's body. The front part is called the thorax.

arachnid
The family of creatures to which spiders belong. Other arachnids include scorpions, mites and ticks.

arachnophobia
(A-rak-no-fobe-ee-ya). Word that describes being terrified of spiders.

burrow
A hole in the ground where a spider or other creature lives.

camouflage
Colours and patterns that allow animals to blend into their surroundings, helping them to hide.

cocoon
A bag of silk used for keeping eggs, or to wrap up prey.

cuticle
A spider's old skin, left after moulting. The cuticle is an exoskeleton (outside skeleton) because spiders have no bones inside their bodies.

fangs
Sharp teeth used to bite prey. Venom is injected through a tube in each fang. Most spiders bite sideways, but tarantulas are different – they bite up and down, like humans.

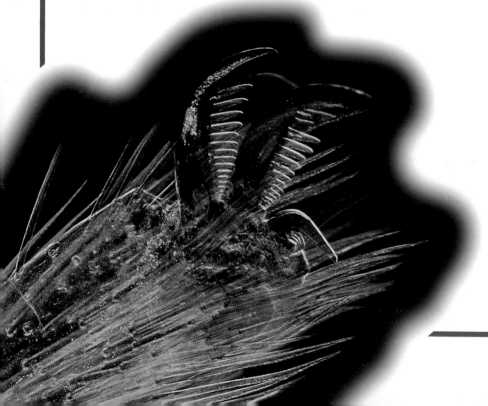

◄ Hooks on their feet let spiders grip slender web threads. Many spiders have foot pads to walk up walls and across ceilings.

hammock web
Web slung between two twigs or plants.

moulting
Breaking out of old skin. After moulting, a spider stays quiet for a while, until its new skin has hardened.

▲ Red-knee tarantula, with old skin on the right.

orb web
Wheel-shaped web made by orb web spiders.

paralyzed
Unable to move – the state of a spider's prey after being bitten and injected with venom.

prey
Any creature that is hunted by another for food.

safety or drag line
A thread of silk behind a spider as it drops or jumps. The line is also used to climb up again.

silk
The thread made by spiders. Spiders often recycle silk – orb spiders eat webs after a day or two, then make new ones.

species
A group of living things that can breed among themselves, and have young that can do the same. There are 35 000 known species of spider.

spiderling
A baby spider, after it has hatched from the egg.

spinneret
One of the tubes at the back of a spider's body, through which silk is released.

tarantula
Name now used for any big, hairy spider. The original tarantula was actually a wolf spider from southern Europe.

venom
Another word for poison. Spider venom turns a prey's insides to mush, which the spider sucks up as food.

◄ Close-up view of a spider's spinnerets.

SPIDER PROJECTS

Making a spider file, with photographs, notes and sketches, will help you find out more about these amazing creatures.

◀ You have to get very close to take good spider photos. Some cameras have a special 'macro' lens setting, designed for close-up shots.

The best place to see a tarantula is in a zoo, or sometimes in a pet shop. But the spiders around your house are worth looking at too – as you can see from the pictures here.

Collect your facts in a spider file – take photographs and make sketches, to add interest. Look out for news stories about spiders.

▲ You need a camera with a macro lens for best results.

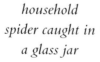

▶ If you catch specimens, release them unharmed.

household spider caught in a glass jar

30

TWEAKING AND SLIDING

These two experiments show you some of the secrets of web spiders.

First, you can use a rubber band to feel how a spider detects something that gets stuck in its web.

The second experiment helps you see why spiders don't stick to their own sticky webs – the secret is the oil that moistens their feet.

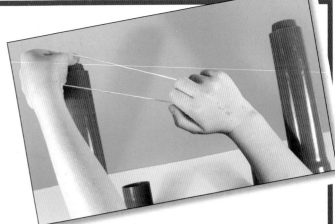

1 Stretch a rubber band between two firm uprights. Here we used the upturned legs of a study plastic table.

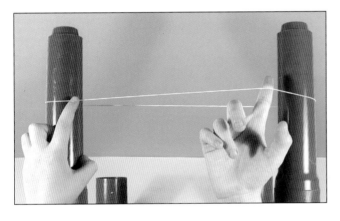

2 Lay a finger of your left hand gently on the rubber 'web'. Pluck the other end with your right hand – and feel the tell-tale vibrations!

3 For the sticky experiment you need some tape and a drop of cooking oil. Pour the oil into a bowl to avoid spills.

4 Cut two short strips of tape, and see how your finger gets sticks to the sticky side of the tape – just like a fly on a web.

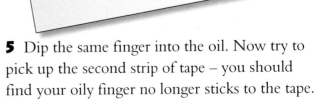

5 Dip the same finger into the oil. Now try to pick up the second strip of tape – you should find your oily finger no longer sticks to the tape.

INDEX